LEVEL I

SOMETHING NEW TO SING ABOUT

CHORAL LITERATURE for MIXED VOICES

Developed by G. SCHIRMER, Inc.
Will Schmid, Project Editor

GLENCOE

Macmillan/McGraw-Hill

Lake Forest, Illinois   Columbus, Ohio   Mission Hills, California   Peoria, Illinois

WRITING TEAM

Will Schmid, Project Editor
University of Wisconsin-Milwaukee

Lee Jacobi, Choral Director
Muskego High School, WI

Richard Larson, Choral Director
Cherry Creek High School, Denver, CO

Wayne Crannell, Project Assistant
University of Wisconsin-Milwaukee

MUSIC SELECTION COMMITTEE

John Scarcella, Director of Music
Cypress Fairbanks School District, Houston, TX

Judy Stephenson, Choral Director
John Marshall High School, San Antonio, TX

Dr. Richard Sutch, Coordinator of Fine Arts
Austin Independent School District, TX

Ralph Zecchino, Choral Director
Greece Arcadia High School, Rochester, NY

IMC
MT875
S645
Gr 9+12
Level-1

Send all inquiries to:
GLENCOE DIVISION
Macmillan/McGraw-Hill
15319 Chatsworth Street
P.O. Box 9609
Mission Hills, CA 91346-9609

ISBN 0-02-642100-3 (Student Text)
ISBN 0-02-642101-1 (Choral Literature, Level I, For Mixed Voices)
ISBN 0-02-642102-X (Choral Literature, Level I, For Treble Ensemble)
ISBN 0-02-642103-8 (Choral Literature, Level II, For Mixed Voices)
ISBN 0-02-642104-6 (Choral Literature, Level II, For Treble Ensemble and Male
              Ensemble)
ISBN 0-02-642105-4 (Choral Literature, Level III, For Mixed Voices)
ISBN 0-02-642106-2 (Choral Literature, Level III, For Treble Ensemble and Male
              Ensemble)
ISBN 0-02-642111-9 (Teacher's Manual and Resources)

Printed in the United States of America.

3 4 5 6 7 8 9 10 11 12 13 14 15   99 98 97 96 95 94 93 92 91

CONTENTS

Alleluia (Cantata 142)

Composer: Johann Sebastian Bach (1685-1750). Some of his best known works: *B Minor Mass, St. Matthew Passion, Brandenburg Concertos* and *Art of the Fugue*.

Type of piece: This piece is the final chorale from *Cantata 142* ("Uns ist ein Kind Geboren"). It has been discovered that this cantata was actually written by Bach's contemporary, Johann Kuhnau.

Historical Traditions: This chorale is drawn from a **cantata**. The cantata is an extended choral work, usually on a religious text, written for soloists, chorus, and orchestra. Composers frequently used chorale melodies as the basis for these compositions.

Text: The cantata, *Uns ist ein Kind Geboren* (Unto us a Child is Born), was written for Christmas.

Key/Scale: A minor.

Texture: Homophonic with independent accompaniment.

Workout

All clap line #1; then half clap line #1 while half clap line #2.

Self-Study Ideas

°Compare the Bach "Alleluia" to other settings such as the "Alleluia" from *Exultate Jubilate* by W. A. Mozart or the choral setting, "Alleluia," by Randall Thompson.

Alleluia

Duration: 1 min. 15 sec.

English version by
Walter Ehret

JOHANN SEBASTIAN BACH
Edited and Piano Realization by Walter Ehret

Allegro

PIANO
or
ORGAN

SOPRANO

Al - le - lu - ia,
Al - le - lu - ja,

ALTO

Al - le - lu - ia,
Al - le - lu - ja,

TENOR

Al - le - lu - ia,
Al - le - lu - ja,

BASS

Al - le - lu - ia,
Al - le - lu - ja,

5

ALLELUIA — SATB

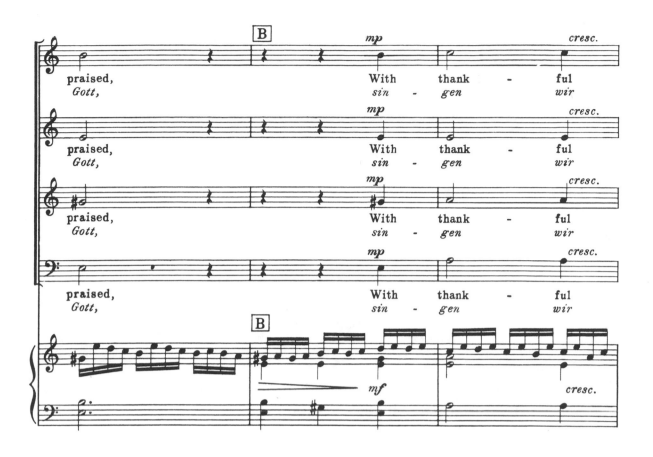

ALLELUIA — SATB

prais - es;
Grun - de;

prais - es;
Grun - de;

prais - es;
Grun - de;

prais - es;
Grun - de;

For God to - day
Denn Gott hat heut'

For God to - day
Denn Gott hat heut'

For God to - day
Denn Gott hat heut'

For God to - day
Denn Gott hat heut'

grate - ful hearts for - get Him _____ nev -
ges - sen soll'n zu kei - ner _____ Stun -

grate - ful hearts for - get Him _____ nev -
ges - sen soll'n zu kei - ner _____ Stun -

grate - ful hearts for - get Him _____ nev -
ges - sen soll'n zu kei - ner _____ Stun -

grate - ful hearts for - get Him _____ nev -
ges - sen soll'n zu kei - ner _____ Stun -

er.
de.

er.
de.

er.
de.

er.
de.

ALLELUIA — SATB

10

And the Glory of the Lord from *Messiah*

Composer: George Frideric Handel (1685-1759). Best known works: *Water Music* (orchestra), *Royal Fireworks Music* (orchestra), *Judas Maccabaeus* (oratorio).

Type of piece: Chorus from sacred oratorio, *Messiah*.

Historical Traditions: Handel was a German Baroque composer who moved to Italy and later England. *Messiah* is probably the most beloved large choral work of all time.

Text: From the Old Testament, Isaiah 40:5.

Key/Scale: A major.

Rhythm: 3/4 *Allegro* (fast).

Texture: Imitative with homophonic sections.

Melody and Form: There are four different melodic themes interwoven throughout the piece. A theme: "And the glory"; B theme: "shall be revealed"; C theme: "and all flesh . . ."; D theme: "For the mouth . . ."

Workout

Continue this pattern up to the octave. Gradually increase the speed.

Do	Do	Re	Do	Do	Re	Mi	Re	Do	Do	Re	Mi	Fa	Mi	Re
1	1	2	1	1	2	3	2	1	1	2	3	4	3	2

Self-Study Ideas

°Listen to a recording of other sections of the *Messiah* such as "Hallelujah Chorus" or the solo aria, "He Shall Feed His Flock."

° Listen to the *Magnificat* by J.S. Bach (1685-1750), a contemporary of Handel.

And The Glory Of The Lord

No. 4. Chorus
From "The Messiah"

For Four - Part Chorus of Mixed Voices
with Piano Accompaniment

Isaiah xl., 5

George Frideric Handel

shall be re - veal - ed,

veal - ed, And the glo - ry, the glo - ry of the

shall be re - veal - ed, shall be re -

and the glo-ry, the glo-ry of the Lord shall

shall be re - veal - ed, be re - veal - - -

Lord shall be re - veal - ed,

veal-ed,

be re - veal'd, and the glo - ry, the glo - ry of the Lord shall be

- - ed, and the glo - ry, the glo - ry of the Lord shall be

and the glo - ry, the glo - ry of the Lord shall be

and the glo - ry, the glo - ry of the Lord shall be

re - veal - ed,

re - veal - ed,   and all

re - veal - ed,

re - veal - ed,

15

21

Cantate Domino

Composer: Giuseppe Pitoni (1657-1743).

Type of piece: Choral setting of a Psalm.

Historical Traditions: Pitoni was a Baroque composer who wrote in an older style using only voices.

Key/Scale: G minor.

Rhythm: Feel in one beat per measure.

Texture: Homophonic with a brief section of imitation.

Form: Through-composed.

Workout

Divide the choir into 2 parts. Sing on a neutral syllable.

Self-Study Ideas

°Listen to "Cantate Domino" by Hans Leo Hassler. How are these two pieces alike or different?

°Read the Psalms as some of the most interesting poetry ever written.

Cantate Domino
(Sing To The Lord, Our God)

For Four-Part Chorus of Mixed Voices
a cappella

English translation by James Pruett

Giuseppi Ottavio Pitoni (1657-1743)
Edited and arranged by John Reed

25

28

Chester

Composer: William Billings (1746-1800).

Type of piece: American hymn-tune.

Historical Traditions: William Billings was a significant American composer during the American Revolution. He is best known for composing a number of **fuguing tunes** as well as many psalm tunes. The piece "Chester" captures the defiant spirit of the American Revolution.

Text: The text illustrates a combination of sacred and patriotic ideas.

Key/Scale: D major.

Melody: This vigorous, sturdy melody is typical of Billings' style.

Rhythm: Feel in 2 beats per measure.

Texture: Homophonic.

Workout

Sing with detachment. Work for abdominal support, and sing with an unforced tone.

Ho ho ho ho ho ho ho ho ho ho ho._____

Move up and down by half steps.

Self-Study Ideas

°Read an essay by Revolutionary American author Thomas Paine.

°Listen to *New England Triptych* and *Chester* (overture for band) by William Schuman.

Chester

For Four-Part Chorus of Mixed Voices
a cappella

William Billings (1746 - 1800)
Arranged by Don Gustafson

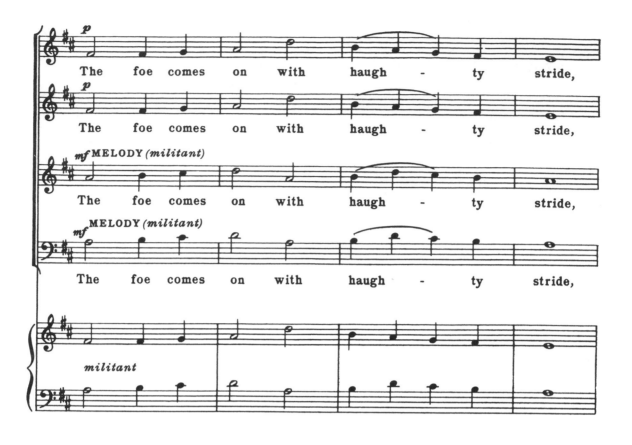

The foe comes on with haugh - ty stride,

The foe comes on with haugh - ty stride,

mf MELODY *(militant)*

The foe comes on with haugh - ty stride,

mf MELODY *(militant)*

The foe comes on with haugh - ty stride,

militant

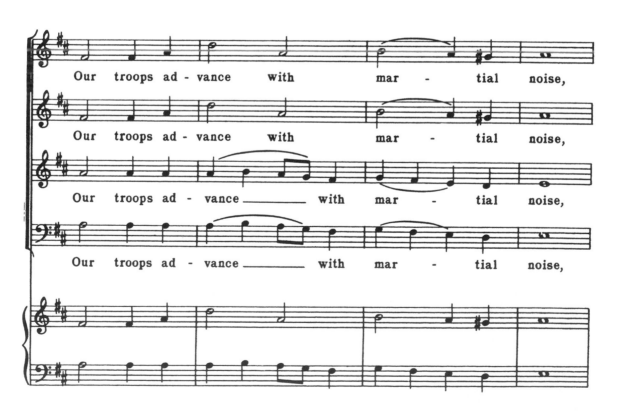

Our troops ad - vance with mar - tial noise,

Our troops ad - vance with mar - tial noise,

Our troops ad - vance _____ with mar - tial noise,

Our troops ad - vance _____ with mar - tial noise,

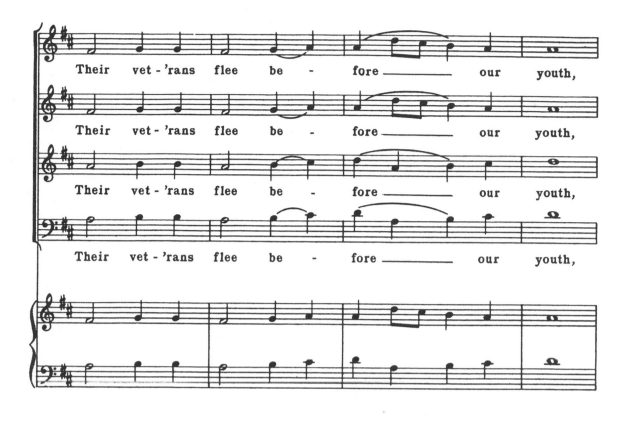

Their vet-'rans flee be - fore ——— our youth,

Their vet-'rans flee be - fore ——— our youth,

Their vet-'rans flee be - fore ——— our youth,

Their vet-'rans flee be - fore ——— our youth,

And gen-'rals yield to beard - less boys.

And gen-'rals yield to beard - less boys.

And — gen-'rals yield ——— to beard - less boys.

And — gen-'rals yield ——— to beard - less boys.

33

What grate-ful off - 'ring shall we bring,

What grate-ful off - 'ring shall we bring,

What grate-ful off - 'ring shall we bring,

What grate-ful off - 'ring shall we bring,

What shall we ren - der to the Lord?

What shall we ren - der to the Lord?

What shall we ren - der to the Lord?

What shall we ren - der to the Lord?

Loud hal - le - lu - jahs let us sing,

Loud hal - le - lu - jahs let us sing,

Loud hal - le - lu - jahs let us sing,

Loud hal - le - lu - jahs let us sing,

And praise His Name on ev - 'ry chord.

And praise His Name on ev - 'ry chord.

And praise His Name on ev - 'ry chord.

And praise His Name on ev - 'ry chord.

Ecce Quam Bonum (See How Good, How Right)

Composer: Jean Richafort (1480-1548).

Type of piece: A short Renaissance motet.

Historical Traditions: The motet is a sacred, polyphonic composition usually sung in Latin.

Text: This piece is a setting of Psalm 133. The text is positive and joyful, ending with an alleluia.

Key/Scale: G major.

Texture: Imitative polyphony.

Workout

4-Part Round

Self-Study Ideas

°Speak the text of "In Pride of May" by Thomas Weelkes (Volume I-Mixed) in rhythm. Sense the imitation.

°Listen to "And the Glory of the Lord" from *Messiah* by G. F. Handel.

Ecce Quam Bonum
(See How Good, How Right)

For Four-Part Chorus of Mixed Voices
a cappella

PSALM 133
Adapted by M. K.

JEAN RICHAFORT
(c. 1480-1548)
Edited by Maynard Klein

The Falcon

Composer: Mary Lynn Baderak (contemporary).

Type of piece: Sad contemporary madrigal written for three voices (SAB).

Key/Scale: D-flat major.

Melody: The melody is gentle and lyrical. The tune first appears in the soprano, and all the parts eventually sing it.

Text: A metaphorical text with many possible meanings. The text contains medieval images of death.

Rhythm: Smooth and gentle.

Texture: Imitative with some paired voicing and inversion.

Form: Through-composed.

Workout

Continue this pattern up to the octave.

See - ah_____ See - ah_____ See - ah_____ See-

Self-Study Ideas

°Write your interpretation of the meaning of the text.
°Read about metaphors, similes, and analogies. Practice using them in conversations with other people.

The Falcon

For Three-Part Chorus of Mixed Voices
with Piano accompaniment

Mary Lynn Badarak

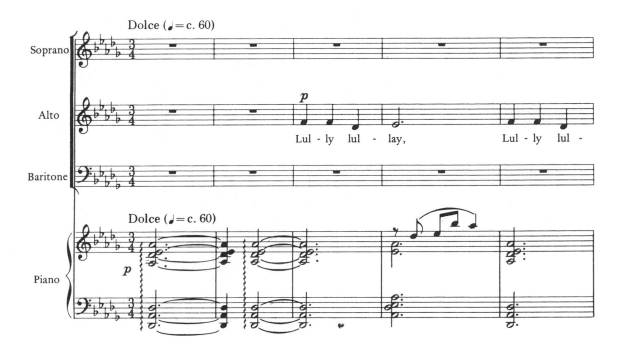

He bare him up _____ He bare_him down, _____ He bare him

in - to an or-chard brown. Lul - ly, _____ Lul - ly lul - lay, _____

Lul - ly lul - lay, Lul - ly lul -

Lul - ly lul - lay, the fal - con hath bourne_ my love a - way. ___

lay, the fal - con hath bourne my love_ a - way. ___

43

44

El Grillo (The Cricket)

Composer: Josquin des Prez (c. 1440-1521).

Type of piece: Early 16th century Italian *frottola*.

Historical Traditions: The *frottola* was the forerunner of the madrigal. It served as the popular music of the 15th and 16th century in Italy.

Key/Scale: G Lydian mode.

Melody: The melody is usually in the soprano, but other sections sing it also.

Text: This humorous Italian text is about the chirping of a cricket.

Rhythm: The rhythm and the voicing imitates the sound of a cricket. Feel this song in 2 beats per measure.

Texture: Homophonic with some paired voicing.

Form: A B A C C D A B. "The Cricket" resembles a rondo in that the A section is repeated.

Workout

Move up by half steps. Gradually increase speed.

dal- le dal- le be - ve be - ve   gril- lo gril-lo can - ta

dal- le dal- le be - ve be - ve   gril- lo gril-lo can - ta   dal.

Self-Study Ideas

°Compare and contrast this *frottola*, "El Grillo," by Josquin des Prez with the madrigal, "In Pride of May," by Thomas Weelkes.

El Grillo
(The Cricket)

For Four-Part Chorus of Mixed Voices
a cappella

Edited and translated by
John Reed

Josquin des Prez
(ca. 1450 - 1521)

ver   -   -   so.
lin   -   -   gers.

ver   -   -   so.
lin   -   -   gers.

ver   -   -   so.
lin   -   -   gers.

ver   -   -   so.
lin   -   -   gers.

1 *mp*

Dal - le   be - ve   gril - lo   can - ta.
By the   riv - er   ev - er   sing - ing.

mp
Dal - le   be - ve   gril - lo   can - ta.
By the   riv - er   ev - er   sing - ing

mp
Dal - le   be - ve   gril - lo   can - ta.
By the   riv - er   ev - er   sing - ing.

mp
Dal - le   be - ve   gril - lo   can - ta.
By the   riv - er   ev - er   sing - ing.

1

to _____ in al - tro lo - co sem - pre el
home _____ and sings for ho - urs fill - ing the

to _____ in al - tro lo - co sem - pre el
home _____ and sings for ho - urs fill - ing the

to _____ in al - tro lo - co sem - pre el
home _____ and sings for ho - urs fill - ing the

to _____ in al - tro lo - co sem - pre el _____
home _____ and sings for ho - urs fill - ing the _____

gril - lo sta pur sal - do, Quan - do la mag -
air with vo - cal flow - ers. When the sum - mer

gril - lo sta pur sal - do, Quan - do la mag -
air with vo - cal flow - ers. When the sum - mer

gril - lo sta pur sal - do, Quan - do la mag -
air with vo - cal flow - ers. When the sum - mer

gril - lo sta pur sal - do, Quan - do la mag -
air with vo - cal flow - ers. When the sum - mer

54

Home On That Rock

Composer: Kirby Shaw (contemporary).

Type of piece: Rock spiritual

Cultural Traditions: Written for one of the best black choirs in this country, the Albert McNeil Jubilee Singers, from California. This piece has its roots in the black gospel tradition.

Key/Scale: F major with blue notes (flatted 3rd and 7th) used at times.

Melody: Chorus: melody in baritone. Verse: melody in soprano.

Harmony: Chorus: SA—parallel thirds—"Home, home"

Rhythm: Syncopation used prominantly. Keep a rock solid steady beat.

Form: Chorus: "Home on . . ."; Verse 1: "When the seas . . ."; Chorus; Verse 2: 'When you're terrified . . ."; Chorus.

Workout

Major Scale   Blues Scale

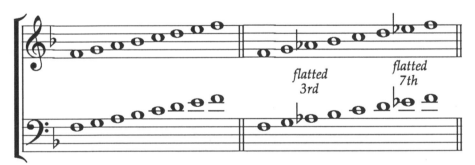

Self-Study Ideas

°Listen to Manhattan Transfer's "Boy from New York City."
°Attend a concert by a black gospel choir or a doo-wop group.

Dedicated to the Albert McNeil Jubilee Singers
Albert F. McNeil, Director

Home On That Rock

SAB† - a cappella

KIRBY SHAW

*small notes optional, sing SSAB meas. 9-14, 36-41, 68-73.

** ♩ = *ascending smear – slide into note from 2-3 steps below. Reach pitch*
just prior to next note or rest. Slight accent.

†Available for:
SATB, SAB, SSA, TBB

© 1981 KIRBY SHAW MUSIC

HOME ON THAT ROCK - SAB

57

HOME ON THAT ROCK, SAB

Home on the Rock! and I'm nev-er gon-na leave it. Home,__

Got a Home__ on that Rock and I'm nev-er gon-na leave it. Home__

__ Home, Home on the Rock!

__ on that Rock! Got a Home__ on that Rock to stay.__

When you're ter-ri-fied__ and want to

__

(foot stomp)

run and hide__ and you're won-drin' just what to do,___ and you

(foot stomp)

blame your-self__ for all the things you've done,__ and who ya been talk-in' to;__

HOME ON THAT ROCK - SAB

60

In Pride of May

Composer/Arranger: Thomas Weelkes (c. 1575-1623). Arranged by Steven Porter.

Type of piece: English Madrigal.

Historical/Cultural Traditions: Weelkes was one of the greatest English madrigal composers. The madrigal was popular during the reign of Queen Elizabeth I. Shakespeare is the best known author of this period.

Text: Nature theme.

Key/Scale: G major

Rhythm: Generally in 2 beats per measure. Meter changes occasionally, but the quarter note remains the same.

Texture: Homophonic with some imitation.

Workout

Self-Study Ideas

°Listen to recordings of English madrigals by the King's Singers. Attend a performance of a collegium musicum at a nearby college or university.

°Read or attend a Shakespearean play such as *As You Like It* or *Measure for Measure*.

In Pride Of May

For Four-Part Chorus of Mixed Voices
(With Optional Piano Accompaniment)

Thomas Weelkes (d. 1623)
Arranged by
STEVEN PORTER

65

Jesu, Joy of Man's Desiring

Composer: Johann Sebastian Bach (1685-1750).

Type of piece: This is a chorale from *Cantata 147* ("Herz und Mund und Tat und Leben"). It was written in 1716 for the Fourth Sunday in Advent.

Historical Traditions: The melody (in the soprano voice) is a German hymn-tune published in 1642.

Text: The text is a good example of a typical chorale.

Key/Scale: G major.

Melody: The melody is built upon ascending and descending scale patterns.

Rhythm: The predominant rhythm is a half note followed by a quarter note.

Texture: Homophonic.

Workout

Shaping the Melody

(Sing on a neutral syllable.)

Sing the melody using these suggestions:
1. *Crescendo when notes go up or are repeated.*
2. *Diminuendo when notes go down and at the last note of the phrase.*

Self-Study Ideas

°Write an expressive melody of your own. Put in appropriate dynamics.
°Find a song and add your own dynamics based on the suggestions in the Workout.

Jesu, Joy Of Man's Desiring
Chorale from Church Cantata No. 147

For Four-Part Chorus of Mixed Voices
with Piano Accompaniment

Johann Sebastian Bach
Arranged by Bryceson Treharne

70

71

72

75

throne.
bricht.
known.
sicht.

throne.
bricht.
known.
sicht.

O Bella Fusa (The Spinning Wheel)

Composer: Orlando di Lasso (1532-1594).

Type of piece: Italian *canzonetta*.

Historical Traditions: A *canzonetta* is a light vocal piece popular in Italy in the late 1500's. They are usually homophonic in texture. The rhythms of the music follow the natural accents of the words.

Text: A light-hearted song which describes the action of a spinning wheel.

Key/Scale: Alternates between D major and A major.

Rhythm: Feel in 2 beats per measure.

Texture: Homophonic with occasional points of imitation.

Workout

Tongue Twisters

Sing the following pattern on each measure alternating the paired consonants in every other measure: Vah vay vee voh voo, Fah, fay, fee, foh, foo—or use these combinations: B-P, G-K, S-Z, T-D.

Self-Study Ideas

°Take a look at Ernst Toch's "Geographical Fugue," an interesting piece based on choral speaking.
°Listen to other Italian *canzonettas* and madrigals with careful attention to how the Italian words are sung.

O Bella Fusa
(The Spinning Wheel)
(Canzonetta)

For Four-Part Chorus of Mixed Voices
a cappella

English text by M. K.

Orlando di Lasso
(1532-1594)

Edited by Maynard Klein

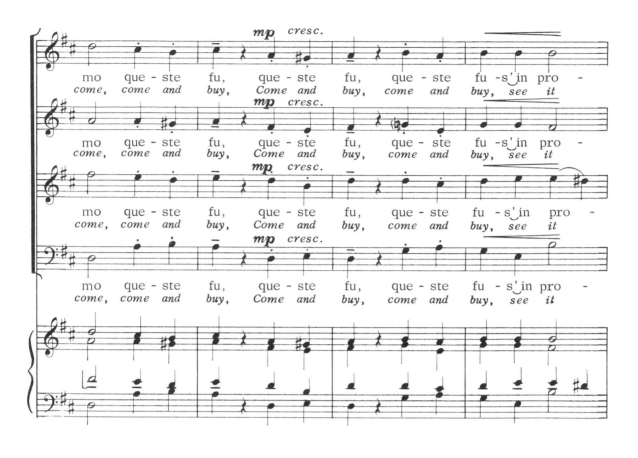

mo que - ste fu, que - ste fu, que - ste fu -s'in pro -
come, come and buy, Come and buy, come and buy, see it

mo que - ste fu, que - ste fu, que - ste fu -s'in pro -
come, come and buy, Come and buy, come and buy, see it

mo que - ste fu, que - ste fu, que - ste fu -s'in pro -
come, come and buy, Come and buy, come and buy, see it

mo que - ste fu, que - ste fu, que - ste fu -s'in pro -
come, come and buy, Come and buy, come and buy, see it

va. Noi le ven - di - mo que - ste fu, que - ste fu, que - ste
go! Will some-one please come, come and buy? Come and buy, see it

va. Noi le ven - di - mo que - ste fu, que - ste fu, que - ste
go! Will some-one please come, come and buy? Come and buy, see it

va. Noi le ven - di - mo que - ste fu, que - ste fu, que - ste
go! Will some-one please come, come and buy? Come and buy, see it

va. Noi le ven - di - mo que - ste fu, que - ste fu, que - ste
go! Will some-one please come, come and buy? Come and buy, see it

81

O Clap Your Hands, All Ye People

Composer: Sonja Poorman (contemporary).

Type of piece: Contemporary psalm setting.

Text: One of the most joyful psalms.

Key/Scale: F major.

Rhythm: Driving and syncopated. Mostly syllabic.

Form: A B A C A Coda. This piece follows a rondo form.

Texture: Homophonic with points of imitation.

Workout

Split into three groups and practice all three parts together.

Self-Study Ideas

°Listen to Ralph Vaughan Williams' "O Clap Your Hands" with brass.

"Text adapted from PSALMS 47:1-2, 5-6; 48:1"

O Clap Your Hands, All Ye People

SATB with Piano Accompaniment

By SONJA POORMAN

Performance Time: c. 2:20

songs_of joy!_ O clap your hands, all ye peo - ple! His prais - es

songs_of joy!_ O clap your hands, all ye peo - ple! His prais - es

songs of joy!_ O clap your hands, all ye peo - ple! His prais - es

songs of joy!_ O clap your hands, all ye peo - ple! His prais - es

sing. O clap your hands, all ye peo - ple!

sing. Clap your hands, all ye peo - ple!

sing. O clap your hands, all ye peo - ple!

sing. O clap your hands, all ye peo - ple!

O CLAP YOUR HANDS, ALL YE PEOPLE - SATB

O CLAP YOUR HANDS, ALL YE PEOPLE - SATB

Lord, and great - ly to be praised on moun - tains

Lord, and great - ly to be praised on moun - tains

Lord, and great - ly to be praised on moun - tains

Lord, and great - ly to be praised on moun - tains

of His great land, and may our

of His great land, His land, and may our

of His great land, and may our

of His great land, and may our

O CLAP YOUR HANDS, ALL YE PEOPLE - SATB

souls for - ev - er be a - mazed at the ex - cel-len - cy

in the pow - er of His hand,

O CLAP YOUR HANDS, ALL YE PEOPLE - SATB

O CLAP YOUR HANDS, ALL YE PEOPLE - SATB

91

O CLAP YOUR HANDS, ALL YE PEOPLE - SATB

92

O CLAP YOUR HANDS, ALL YE PEOPLE - SATB

O CLAP YOUR HANDS, ALL YE PEOPLE - SATB

94

Praise Ye the Lord of Hosts

Composer: Camille Saint-Saëns (1835-1921). Best known works—*Carnival of the Animals* (orchestra), *Samson et Dalila* (opera), *Danse Macabre* (orchestra).

Type of piece: Sacred chorus from *Christmas Oratorio.*

Historical tradition: 19th century Romantic style.

Key/Scale: G major

Rhythm: *Maestoso* (with majesty), stately. Feel in 2 beats per measure.

Form: A A B B C B.

Texture: AB sections—homophonic. C section—imitative.

Workout

Split into groups and practice all the parts together. Clap or use a "tah."

Self-Study Ideas

°If you heard only the music of this piece (with no words), would you identify it as being sacred or secular?

°What hymns can you find that have a similar style or feeling?

°Listen to *Pomp and Circumstance* by Elgar for a good example of the noble style.

Praise Ye The Lord Of Hosts

From "Christmas Oratorio"

For Four-Part Chorus of Mixed Voices
with Piano Accompaniment

English version by N. H. Dole

Camille Saint-Saëns

heav'ns, and be joy - ful, on earth, re - joice in the face of the
coe - li, et e - xul - tet ter - ra, a fa - ci - e Do - mi-

heav'ns, and be joy - ful, on earth, for He com -
coe - li, et e - xul - tet ter - ra, quo - ni - am ve -

Lord, for He com - eth, Al - le - lu - ia. ia.
ni, quo - ni - am ve - nit. Al - le - lu - ia ia.

eth. Al - le - lu - ia, Al - le - lu - ia. ia. Al - le - lu
nit. Al - le - lu - ia, Al - le - lu - ia. ia. Al - le - lu -

Re - joice, ye an - gels re - joice all ye na - tions,
Loe - ten - tur coe - li, et e - xul - tet ter - ra,

Re - joice, ye an - gels re - joice all ye na - tions,
Loe - ten - tur coe - li, et e - xul - tet ter - ra,

now in the face of the Lord, for He com - eth. Al - le - lu - ia.
a fa - ci - e Do - mi - ni, quo - ni - am ve - nit. Al - le - lu - ia.

for He com - eth. Al - le - lu - ia, Al - le - lu - ia.
quo - ni - am ve - nit. Al - le - lu - ia, Al - le - lu - ia.

Regina Caeli

Composer: Francesco Suriano.

Type of piece: Renaissance setting of a text for Easter.

Historical Traditions: This is a relatively simple setting of a very well-known sacred text.

Key/Scale: G major.

Melody: In the soprano voice.

Rhythm: Feel in a relaxed four beats per measure. The quarter notes in the 3/4 section are twice as fast as the other sections.

Texture: Homophonic with points of imitation.

Form: Through-composed.

Workout

Sing on a neutral syllable, and bring out the points of imitation.

Self-Study Ideas

°Translate the text. Try to set the translation to the music, but feel free to change certain words to make them fit.

°Write a short paper on Francesco Suriano.

Regina Caeli

For Four-Part Chorus of Mixed Voices,
a cappella

FRANCESCO SURIANO
Edited by Steven Porter

ti, por-ta - - - - - - re. Al-le-lu - ia. Al-le-lu - ia.

ti, por-ta - - - - - re. Al-le-lu - ia. Al-le-lu - ia.

ti, por-ta - - - - re. Al-le-lu - ia. Al-le-lu - ia.

ti, por-ta - - - - re. Al-le-lu - ia. Al-le-lu - ia.

Al - le - lu - ia. Si - cut dix - - - - it. Al -

Al - le - lu - ia. Si - cut dix - - - it.

Al - le - lu - ia. Si - cut dix - - - it.

Al - le - lu - ia. Si - cut dix - - it. Al -

Sanctus (Holy, Holy, Holy)

Composer: Wolfgang Amadeus Mozart (1756-1791). Best known works: *Magic Flute* (opera), *Marriage of Figaro* (opera), *Requiem* (chorus/orchestra), 41 symphonies.

Type of piece: Fourth section from *Missa Brevis* (short mass) K. 259.

Historical Traditions: Mozart was one of the best known composers of the Classical Period (1750-1820). This piece was written in 1776 (the same year as the American "Declaration of Independence").

Key/Scale: C major

Melody: In the soprano. Frequent use of *appoggiatura*.

Harmony: Uses mostly the I, IV and V chords.

Rhythm and Form: *Adagio maestoso* (slow and majestic) followed by *Allegro* (fast in 2 beats per measure).

Dynamics: Sudden shifts from loud to soft (terraced dynamics) in both voice and accompaniment parts.

Workout

The Appoggiatura

The circled notes are dissonant—not part of the chord. They are called appoggiaturas, and they resolve to the chord on the second beat of the measure.

Self-Study Ideas

°See the movie *Amadeus*. Listen to the *Requiem*.

Sanctus

(Holy, Holy, Holy)
from "Missa Brevis" in C, K.259

for Mixed Chorus (SATB) and Piano or Organ

Duration: 1 min., 15 sec.

W. A. MOZART
Edited and arranged by John Cramer

* All passages marked "Solo" may be sung instead by the full choir.

Simple Gifts

Arranger: Marie Pooler

Type of piece: Shaker song.

Historical/Cultural Traditions: 19th century American folk hymn of the Shaker sect. Also known under the title, "Lord of the Dance," with new words by Sydney Carter.

Key/Scale: G major (uses only tones 1 2 3 4 5 and 7).

Melody: Sounds a little like a fiddle tune. Binary form—A B original tune had repeated A and B sections.

Harmony: I and V chords are outlined by the melody.

Rhythm: Feel in 2 beats per measure.

Texture: Imitative, polyphonic.

Form: First verse words used 3 times. Section I: SA enter with TB following in imitation. Section II: TB carry the melody. Section III: Closing section develops the opening phrase. Accompaniment—harp-like ostinatos.

Workout

Sing the 3rd of each major triad on the bright (high) side. This is the note B in the tonic chord and the note F# in the dominant chord.

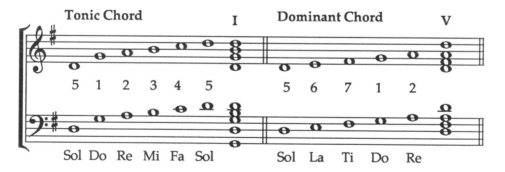

Notice how the melody outlines each of the chords above.

Self-Study Ideas

° Listen to the "Variations on a Shaker Tune" near the end of Aaron Copland's *Appalachian Spring*.

° Check out a book on the Shakers such as Edward D. Andrews' *The Gift to be Simple* or a book on Shaker furniture or art. How is the theme of simplicity woven into all aspects of the Shaker way of life?

Simple Gifts

For Four-Part Chorus of Mixed Voices
with Piano Accompaniment

American Shaker Song
Arranged by Marie Pooler

plic-i-ty is gained, To bow and to bend we shan't be a-shamed, To

plic-i-ty is gained, To bow we shan't be a-shamed, To

true sim-plic-i-ty is gained, we shan't be a-shamed, To

true sim-plic-i-ty is gained, we shan't be a-shamed, To

turn, turn will be our de-light, Till by turn - ing, turn - ing we

turn,— turn will be our de-light, Till by turn - ing, turn - ing we

turn, turn will be our de-light, Till by turn - ing, turn - ing we

turn,— turn will be our de-light, Till by turn - ing, turn - ing we

come round right.

come round right.

come round right.

come round right.

'Tis the gift, gift,

'Tis the gift, gift,

'Tis the gift to be sim-ple, 'tis the

'Tis the gift to be sim-ple, 'tis the

with pedal

114

gift   to be free, 'Tis the gift   to   come down where we ought to be,   And

gift   to be free, 'Tis the gift   to   come   down where we ought to be,   And

gift   to be free, 'Tis the gift   to   be   where   we   should   be,   And

gift   to be free, 'Tis the gift   to   be   where   we   should   be,   And

in   the   place   just_ right, 'Twill   be   in the val - ley of

in   the   place   just   right, 'Twill   be   in the val - ley of

when we find our-selves in the place   just   right, 'Twill   be   in the val - ley of

when we find our-selves in the place   just   right, 'Twill   be   in the val - ley of

love and de-light. When true sim-plic-i-ty is gained, To

love and de-light. When true sim-plic-i-ty is gained, To

love and de-light. When true sim-plic-i-ty is gained, To

love and de-light. When true sim-plic-i-ty is gained, To

bow and to bend we shan't be a-shamed, To turn, turn,

bow and to bend we shan't be a-shamed, To turn, turn,

bow and to bend we shan't be a-shamed, To turn, turn will

bow and to bend we shan't be a-shamed, To turn, turn will

turn in de-light, Till by turn - ing, turn - ing we come round right.

turn in de-light, Till by turn - ing, turn - ing we come round right.

be our de-light, Till by turn - ing, turn - ing we come round right.

be our de-light, Till by turn - ing, turn - ing we come round right.

mp
'Tis the

mp
'Tis the

mp
'Tis the

mp
'Tis the

Six Folk Songs

Composer: Johannes Brahms (1833-1897).

Type of piece: A set of German folksongs in an English translation.

Cultural Traditions: Each of the pieces is a German love song.

Text: Although these songs are love songs, the different texts create a contrasting mood in each.

Key/Scale: Each of the songs is in a contrasting key—F, Am, E, Am, E-flat, and Gm.

Rhythm: Each of the songs is in simple meter. The rhythms of the music flow out of the natural word stresses of the texts.

Texture: All the songs are generally homophonic with the melody kept in the soprano voice.

Form: Each of the songs is an example of strophic form.

Workout

Major/Minor Relationships

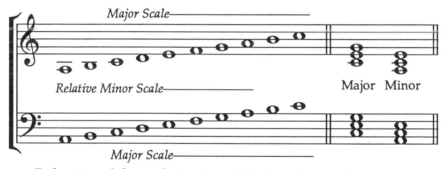

Each major scale has a relative minor which shares the same key signature. The relative minor starts on the 6th tone of the major scale.

Self-Study Ideas

°Create a one-word subtitle for each song based on its text.

°Listen to a number of folk songs. Discover how the words affect the dynamics and moods of the songs. Compare the Brahms' folksongs to songs you already know. What are the similarities and differences?

Six Folk Songs

I'd Enter Your Garden

English Translation by
Harold Heiberg

JOHANNES BRAHMS
Piano score arr. by Herbert Zipper

is their love-liest hour! Since their beau-ty has won me, my heart's in their power.
which I fond-ly sigh__ That your cheeks are the ro - ses, I can - not de - ny.

The Fiddler

Lively, but not too fast

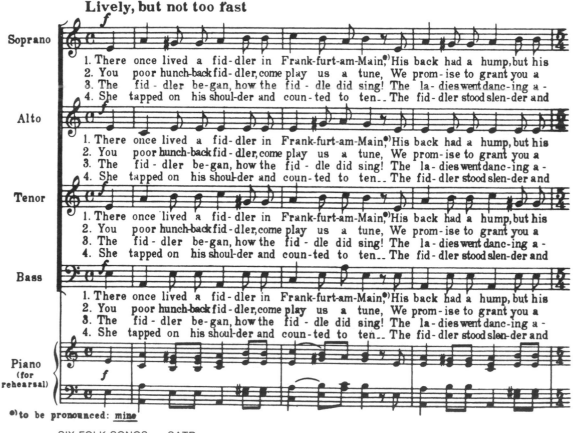

Soprano / Alto / Tenor / Bass

1. There once lived a fid-dler in Frank-furt-am-Main,*) His back had a hump, but his
2. You poor hunch-back fid-dler, come play us a tune, We prom-ise to grant you a
3. The fid - dler be-gan, how the fid - dle did sing! The la-dies went danc-ing a -
4. She tapped on his shoul-der and coun-ted to ten__ The fid - dler stood slen-der and

Piano (for rehearsal)

*)to be pronounced: mine

SIX FOLK SONGS — SATB

SIX FOLK SONGS — SATB

123

How Sad Flow the Streams

At Night

Awake, Awake!

SIX FOLK SONGS — SATB

127

A House Stands 'neath the Willows' Shade

Graceful and lively

SIX FOLK SONGS — SATB

SIX FOLK SONGS — SATB

The Sky Can Still Remember

Composer: Michael A. Gray (contemporary).

Type of piece: Christmas.

Text: By Phillips Brooks, the man who wrote the words to "O Little Town of Bethlehem."

Key/Scale: F-sharp minor

Melody: In the soprano

Rhythm: In 4/4, but should be felt in 2 beats per measure.

Form: Verse 1—unison; Verse 2—3-part harmony.

Workout

F-sharp Melodic Minor

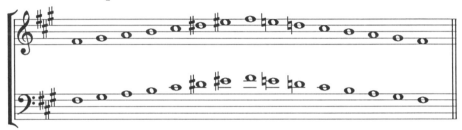

Vocalise   *Sing on a neutral syllable.*

Self-Study Ideas

°Find out something about Phillips Brooks, the author of the words.

°Find and learn other Christmas songs in minor keys. It is often said that pieces in minor keys are "sad." Do you agree or disagree on the basis of the pieces you have found?

The Sky Can Still Remember

For Three-Part Chorus of Mixed Voices
with Piano accompaniment

PHILLIPS BROOKS

MICHAEL A. GRAY

Sustained, but not too slow ♩=112*

The_ sky can still re-mem-ber the ear-liest Christ-mas morn, When_ in the cold De-cem-ber the

*Should be learned in 4/4 but performed in 2/2.

Sav - iour Christ was born. No __ star un - folds its

poco

glo - ry, no trum - pet wind __ is __ blown, But __

mp

tells the Christ - mas sto - ry in mu - sic of its

own.

133

tend-ed the com-ing of the King. Till we too bold-ly

tend-ed the coming of the King. Till we too bold-ly

tend-ed the com-ing of the King. Till we too bold-ly

press-ing where once the shep-herds trod, Climb

press-ing where once the shep-herds trod, Climb

press-ing where once the shep-herds trod, Climb

Beth-l'hems hill of bless-ing and find the Son of

Beth-l'hems hill of bless-ing and find the Son of

Beth-l'hems hill of bless-ing and find the Son of

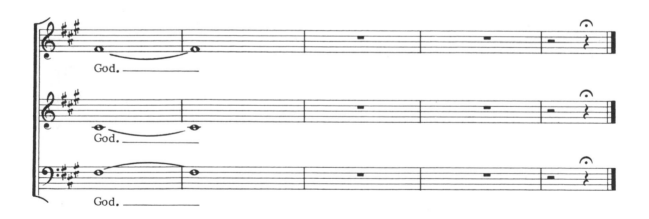

God.

God.

God.

slight rit.

Somewhere Out There

Composer: James Horner, Barry Mann and Cynthia Weil. Arranged by Ed Lojeski.

Type of piece: Popular.

Historical/Cultural Traditions: Song from a movie soundtrack.

Key/Scale: C major

Melody: Graceful arching melody.

Form: A A B A form typical of many popular songs. Coda at the end.

Workout

How many different ways can you sing this phrase?

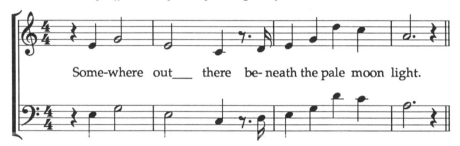

Some-where out___ there be- neath the pale moon light.

Self-Study Ideas

°Listen to Linda Ronstadt sing some of the great American popular songs on her albums: *What's New* and *Lush Life*. Pay particular attention to how she phrases these melodies.

Recorded by LINDA RONSTADT and JAMES INGRAM

Somewhere Out There
From the Universal Motion Picture AN AMERICAN TAIL

For SAB* Voices and Piano with Optional Instrumental Accompaniment

Performance Notes:
This is not a difficult arrangement and can be learned in a relatively
short time. It is preferred that the piano part be played on a Fender
Rhodes piano.

E.L.

Performance Time: Approx. 3:30

Words and Music by
JAMES HORNER,
BARRY MANN and CYNTHIA WEIL

Arranged by
ED LOJESKI

*Available for SATB, SAB, SSA and 2-Part
Instrumental Pak and ShowTrax
Cassette available separately.

when the night wind starts to sing a lone-some lul-la-by   It

poco rit.   *cresc. e molto rit.*   *a tempo*

helps to think we're sleep-ing un-der-neath the same big sky.

34

To Coda

Some-where   out   there   if love   can   see us

SOMEWHERE OUT THERE - SAB

SOMEWHERE OUT THERE - SAB

142

A Song of Hanukkah

Composer: Samuel Adler (contemporary). Professor of composition and theory at the Eastman School of Music.

Type of piece: A setting of the traditional Jewish song from the festival of Hanukkah.

Melody: Moves from voice to voice.

Key/Scale: E natural minor.

Rhythm: With the feel of a folk dance.

Form: Introduction; Verse; Chorus; Verse and Coda.

Workout

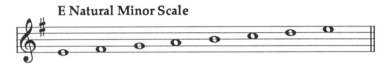

Self-Study Ideas

°Find out more about Hanukkah. What is the significance of the Menorah candles?

°Listen to Ernest Bloch's *Schelomo* for cello and orchestra.

A Song Of Hanukkah
(The Feast Of Lights)

For Four-Part Chorus of Mixed Voices
with Piano Accompaniment

E. Guthmann

Samuel Adler

From Ⓐ to Ⓑ may be sung unaccompanied

Translation courtesy of the Jewish Education Committee of New York.

*"draydel"– a spinning top

all week long; Tell the age-old sto - ry, Sing a hap-py song.

all week long; Tell the age-old sto - ry, Sing a hap-py song.

Ah, And

Ah, And

Ha-nuk-kah, Ha-nuk-kah, Ha-nuk-kah, Ha - nuk-kah, Ha-nuk-kah, Ha-nuk-kah, Ha-

Ha-nuk-kah, Ha-nuk-kah, Ha-nuk-kah, Ha - nuk-kah, Ha-nuk-kah, Ha-nuk-kah, Ha-

while we are sing - ing, The can - dles are burn - ing

while we are sing - ing, The can - dles are burn - ing

shed a sweet light, To re - mind us of days long a - go. O

shed a sweet light, To re - mind us of days long a - go. O

shed a sweet light, To re - mind us of days long a - go. O

shed a sweet light, To re - mind us of days long a - go. O

Ha - nuk - kah, O Ha - nuk - kah, a fes - ti - val of joy;— A

Ha - nuk - kah, O Ha - nuk - kah, a fes - ti - val of joy;— A

Ha - nuk - kah, O Ha - nuk - kah, a fes - ti - val of joy;— A

Ha - nuk - kah, O Ha - nuk - kah, a fes - ti - val of joy;— A

hol - i - day, a jol - ly day for ev - 'ry girl and boy.__ Spin the whirl-ing dray-del

hol - i - day, a jol - ly day for ev - 'ry girl and boy.__ Spin the whirl-ing dray-del

hol - i - day, a jol - ly day for ev - 'ry gir and boy.__ Spin the whirl-ing dray-del

hol - i - day, a jol - ly day for ev - 'ry gir and boy.__

all week_long. Tell the age old sto - ry, Sing a hap - py

all week_long.__ Tell the age old sto - ry,_ Sing a hap - py

all week_long.__ Tell the age old sto - ry, Sing a hap-py song.

Tell the age old sto - ry, Sing a hap-py song.

149

song. Ha-nuk-kah, Ha-nuk-kah, Ha-nuk-kah, Ha-nuk-kah, Ha-nuk-kah, Ha-nuk-

song. Ha-nuk-kah, Ha-nuk-kah, Ha-nuk-kah, Ha-nuk-kah, Ha-nuk-kah, Ha-nuk-

Ha-nuk-kah, Ha-nuk-kah, Ha - nuk-kah, Ha-nuk-kah, Ha-nuk-kah,

Ha-nuk-kah, Ha-nuk-kah, Ha - nuk-kah, Ha-nuk-kah, Ha-nuk-kah,

kah, Ha - nuk-kah, _____ Ha-nuk-kah.

kah, Ha - nuk-kah, _____ Ha-nuk - kah.

Ha - nuk - kah, Ha-nuk - kah, Ha-nuk-kah, Ha-nuk - kah.

Ha - nuk - kah, Ha-nuk - kah, Ha-nuk-kah, Ha-nuk - kah.

This Little Light of Mine

Arranger: Arthur Frackenpohl (contemporary).

Type of piece: Black spiritual.

Historical/Cultural Traditions: The black spiritual tradition grew out of the 19th century Great Revival—a religious movement that spread across the country.

Text: A combination of various black spiritual/gospel texts.

Key/Scale: G major/A-flat major.

Melody: Primarily major pentatonic: D E G A B

Rhythm: Lively. Feel in 2 beats per measure. Lots of syncopation.

Form: M. 5—melody I; M. 21—melody II; M. 37—melody III; M. 53—combines melodies I and II; M. 73—melody III with underlying long-note accompaniment; M. 89—combines melodies I and II; M. 105—Coda.

Workout

Self-Study Ideas

°Listen to Aretha Franklin, Mahalia Jackson, Ray Charles, or James Brown sing the black style full of syncopation and improvisation.

°Make up new verses to the melody I such as: "All around the world, I'm gonna let it shine."

This Little Light Of Mine

For SATB Voices and Piano

Performance Time: Approx. 1:45

Traditional
Arranged by
ARTHUR FRACKENPOHL

THIS LITTLE LIGHT OF MINE — SATB

glo-ry to Your Fa-ther who is in heav-en.

Unis.
mf

1. The

37 Unis.
mp

Ah,

light that shines is the light of love,— lights the dark-ness from a - bove, It

Ah,   Ah,

shines on me and it shines on you,— and shows what the pow-er of love can do; I'm gon-na

THIS LITTLE LIGHT OF MINE — SATB

shine my light both far and near, I'm gon - na shine my light both

bright and clear,___ where there's a dark cor - ner in this land__ I'm gon - na

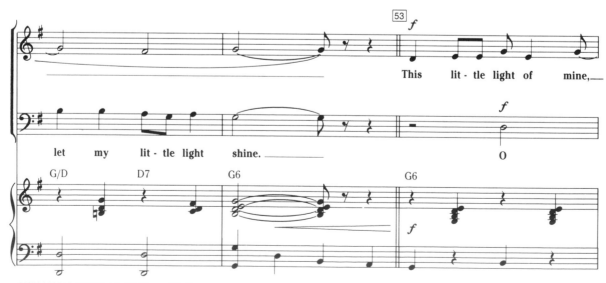

let my lit - tle light shine. _____ This lit - tle light of mine,___

I'm gon-na let it shine,

You are the light of the world,

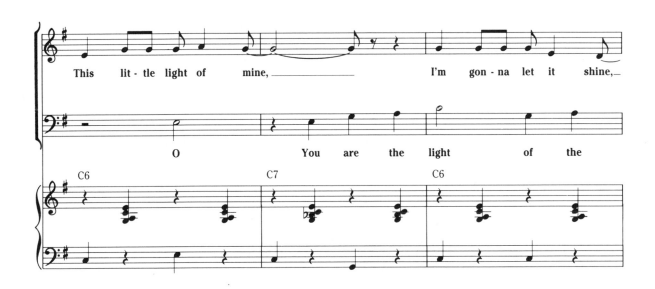

This lit-tle light of mine, I'm gon-na let it shine,

O You are the light of the

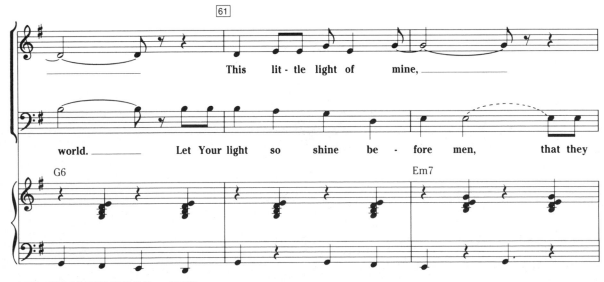

This lit-tle light of mine,

world. Let Your light so shine be-fore men, that they

THIS LITTLE LIGHT OF MINE — SATB

157

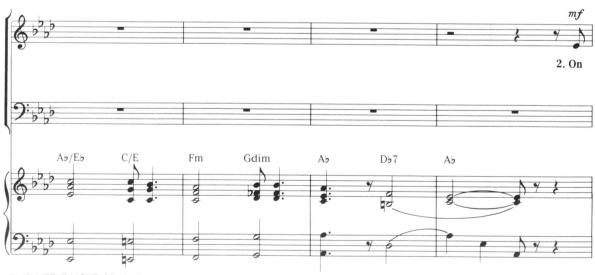

THIS LITTLE LIGHT OF MINE — SATB

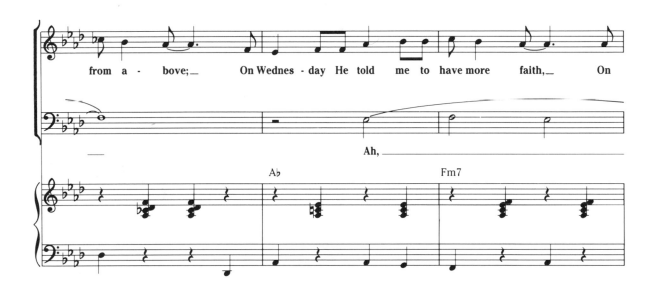

THIS LITTLE LIGHT OF MINE — SATB

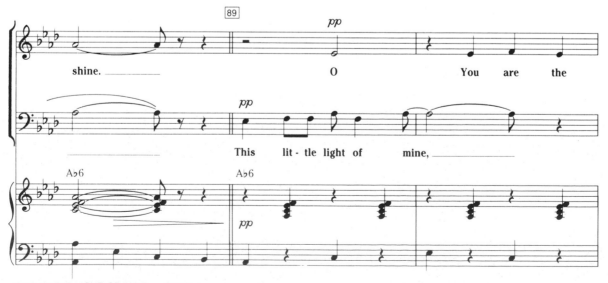

THIS LITTLE LIGHT OF MINE — SATB

THIS LITTLE LIGHT OF MINE — SATB

161

works, and give glo-ry to Your Fa-ther who is in

Let it shine, let it shine, let it

heav-en. This lit-tle light of mine,

shine!

let it shine!

THIS LITTLE LIGHT OF MINE — SATB

162

Three Choral Songs

Composer: L. A. Christiansen (contemporary).

Type of piece: A set of three short songs for choir.

Key/Scale: E minor/A minor. The pieces move between those keys.

Text: These selections are set to varied texts by Robert Lewis Stevenson, L. A. Christiansen, and Solomon.

Texture: The songs are mostly homophonic with a few points of independence.

Form: Each piece is through-composed. Overall, the set is slow—fast—slow.

Workout

Choral Warmup

Slowly change chords and listen for tuning.

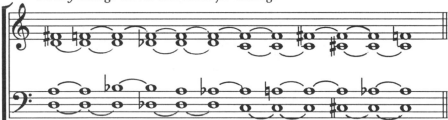

Self-Study Ideas

°Compare and contrast "Six Folk Songs" by Johannes Brahms with "Three Choral Songs."

°Choose three short fragments of poetry by different authors which you think would make a good set of songs.

Three Choral Songs

For Four-Part Chorus of Mixed Voices
a cappella

L. A. Christiansen, Opus 23

1. Let Beauty Awake

R. L. Stevenson

2. Dance With Me

L. A. C.

3. Arise, My Love, My Fair One

Solomon

A - rise my love, my fair one and come a - way;— for

lo, the win - ter is past,— the rain is gone and

flow'rs have ap - pear'd, and birds are heard through the land. A -

rise, my love, and come a - way, a - way.

When I Was One-and-Twenty

Composer: Robert Rhein (contemporary).

Type of piece: Choral part-song.

Text: A setting of a poem by A. E. Housman, a well-known English poet.

Key/Scale: D major.

Melody: A jaunty, folk-like tune.

Rhythm: Feel in 2 beats per measure.

Texture: Homophonic.

Workout

Self-Study Ideas

°Read other poems by A. E. Housman.
°Listen to recordings of English folksongs and ballads.

for Mia Durham

Three Songs from "A Shropshire Lad"

3. When I Was One-and-Twenty

for Three-Part Chorus of Mixed Voices
with Piano Accompaniment

A.E. Housman
(1859–1936)

Robert Rhein

169

I was one - and - twen - ty, No use to talk to__ me.

I was one - and - twen - ty,___ No use to talk to__ me.

I was one - and - twen - ty,___ No use to talk to me.

When

When

When

paid with sighs a - plen - ty And sold for __ end - less __ rue." And

paid with sighs a - plen - ty And sold for __ end - less rue." And

paid with sighs a - plen - ty And sold __ for __ end - less rue." And

Suddenly slower ♩ = 60

I am two - and - twen - ty, And oh, 'tis true, 'tis __

I am two - and - twen - ty, And oh, __ 'tis true, 'tis __

I am two - and - twen - ty, And oh, 'tis true, 'tis __

Suddenly slower ♩ = 60

true.

true.

true.

Calmly   (not at tempo I)

dim.

pp

With a Voice of Singing

Composer: Martin Shaw (1875-1958). English organist.

Type of piece: Choral anthem—majestic and festive.

Text: General praise with alleluias.

Key/Scale: C major/E major/C major.

Rhythm: Feel in 2 beats per measure. The ♪♪♩ ♩ rhythm predominates in the alleluia sections and is passed from voice to voice.

Texture: Mostly homophonic with imitative alleluias.

Form: A B A with small coda.

Workout

Sing in sections with entrances at intervals of 2 or 4 beats.
Alternate the order of section entrances.

La la la   la   la   la

Self-Study Ideas

°Listen to William Walton's *Crown Imperial March* for a good example of the majestic style found in this anthem.

°The rhythms used in the alleluia sections are also found in Bach's *Brandenburg Concerto, No.2*, 1st mvt.

Dedicated to G. Hylton Stewart
Composed for the 1923 Annual Festival of the
Rochester Diocesan Church Choirs Association

With A Voice Of Singing

Martin Shaw

Orchestra parts available on rental from the publishers.

Lord hath de - liv - er - ed his peo - ple, Al - le -

Lord hath de - liv - er - ed his peo - ple, Al -

Lord hath de - liv - er - ed his peo - ple,

Lord hath de - liv - er - ed his peo - ple,

lu - ia. The Lord hath de -

- le - lu - ia. The Lord hath de -

Al - le - lu - ia. The Lord hath de -

Al - le - lu - ia. The Lord hath de -

liv - er - ed his peo - ple, Al - le - lu - ia,

liv - er - ed his peo - ple, Al - le -

liv - er - ed his peo - ple, Al - le - lu -

liv - er - ed his peo - ple, Al -

Al - le - lu - ia.

lu - ia, Al - le - lu - ia.

ia, Al - le - lu - ia.

- le - lu - ia, Al - le - lu - ia.

O be joy-ful in God, all ye lands,

O be joy-ful in God, all ye lands,

O be joy-ful in God, all ye lands,

O be joy-ful in God, all ye lands,

O sing prais-es to the hon-or of his

O sing prais-es to the hon-or of his

O sing prais-es to the hon-or of his

O sing prais-es to the hon-or of his

name, make his praise to be glo - - rious.

With a voice of sing - ing de-clare ye this, and let it be

With a voice of sing - ing de-clare ye this, and let it be

With a voice of sing - ing de-clare ye this, and let it be

With a voice of sing - ing de-clare ye this, and let it be

heard, Al - le - lu - ia.

heard, Al - le - lu - ia. De-clare ye

heard, Al - le - lu - ia. De-clare ye this, and

heard, Al - le - lu - ia.

184

Won't You Charleston With Me?

Composer: Sandy Wilson (contemporary). Arranged by Mac Huff.

Type of piece: Song from the musical, *The Boyfriend*. This is a dance piece.

Historical/Cultural Traditions: Broadway musical. The Charleston was a popular dance done by "the flappers" of the "roaring 20's." The Charleston grew out of the syncopated style of ragtime.

Key/Scale: C major.

Melody: Angular; grows out of chord tones.

Rhythm: Highly syncopated. A toe-tapper.

Form: Verse; Chorus (repeated); Coda.

Workout

Can you tap two of these rhythms at the same time?

Self-Study Ideas

°Ask your grandparents or other older acquaintances about the "Roaring 20's." What was life like, and what other dances did they do?

°Listen to the ragtime music of Scott Joplin or the early piano jazz of Fats Waller and Jelly Roll Morton.

From "THE BOYFRIEND"

Won't You Charleston With Me?

For SATB* Voices with Piano and Optional Instrumental Accompaniment

Performance Time: Approx. 2:12

Arranged by
MAC HUFF

Music and Lyrics by
SANDY WILSON

*Available for SATB and SAB
Instrumental Pak includes Trumpet 1 and 2,
Tenor Sax, Trombone, Guitar, Bass and Drums
ShowTrax Cassette also available

*pronounced (egg - o)
WON'T YOU CHARLESTON WITH ME? - SATB

WON'T YOU CHARLESTON WITH ME? - SATB

189

Charles - ton, __ Charles - ton __ with me.

We'll show you how the __ Charles - is

done. __ We'll sur - prise ev - 'ry - one.

WON'T YOU CHARLESTON WITH ME? - SATB